DEC 2006

A Robbie Reader

What's So
Great About...?
HENRY HUDSON

Carol Parenzan Smalley

P.O. Box 196
Hockessin, Delaware 19707
Visit us on the web: www.mitchelllane.com
Comments? email us: mitchelllane@mitchelllane.com

Printing　　　1　　　2　　　3　　　4　　　5　　　6　　　7　　　8　　　9

A Robbie Reader/What's So Great About . . . ?

Annie Oakley	Daniel Boone	Davy Crockett
Ferdinand Magellan	Francis Scott Key	**Henry Hudson**
Jacques Cartier	Johnny Appleseed	Robert Fulton
Sam Houston		

Library of Congress Cataloging-in-Publication Data
Smalley, Carol Parenzan, 1960–
　　Henry Hudson / by Carol Parenzan Smalley.
　　　　p. cm. — (A Robbie Reader. What's So Great About . . . ?)
　　Includes bibliographical references and index.
　　ISBN 1-58415-479-9 (library bound: alk. paper)
　　1. Hudson, Henry, d. 1611 — Travel — Juvenile literature. 2. America — Discovery and exploration — English — Juvenile literature. 3. Explorers — America — Biography — Juvenile literature. 4. Explorers — Great Britain — Biography — Juvenile literature. I. Title. II. Series.
E129.H8S63 2006
910.92 — dc22
　　　　　　　　　　　　　　　　　　　　　　　　　　　　　　　　　　　2005028509
ISBN–10: 1-58415-479-9　　　　　　　　　ISBN–13: 978-1-58415-479-2

ABOUT THE AUTHOR: Carol Parenzan Smalley loves to explore. She studied water and waterways at The Pennsylvania State University. She lives in upstate New York in a log cabin, about an hour from the Hudson River, where Henry Hudson sailed the *Half Moon*.

PHOTO CREDITS: Cover, pp. 1, 3, 4 — Getty Images; p. 6 — Andrea Pickens; p. 8 — North Wind Picture Archives; p. 11 — Andrea Pickens; p. 12 — Getty Images; p. 14 — Andrea Pickens; p. 15 — Getty Images; p. 17 — Corbis; p. 18 — North Wind Picture Archives; p. 20 — Getty Images; pp. 22, 23, 24 — North Wind Picture Archives; p. 26 — Getty Images

ACKNOWLEDGMENTS: The following story has been thoroughly researched, and to the best of our knowledge represents a true story. While every possible effort has been made to ensure accuracy, the publisher will not assume liability for damages caused by inaccuracies in the data, and makes no warranty on the accuracy of the information contained herein.

PLB

TABLE OF CONTENTS

Words in **bold** type can be found in the glossary.

English explorer Henry Hudson set sail four times between 1607 and 1610 to find a new ocean passageway to the Orient, the eastern part of Asia. On his journeys, he discovered the Hudson River in New York State, and the Hudson Bay and Hudson Strait in Canada.

A Mysterious Sailor

Little is known about Henry Hudson. **Historians** know he was from London, England, but they do not know when he was born. It may have been around 1570.

They are not sure of the names of his parents. His father may have also been called Henry Hudson. They do know the names of his four brothers: Christopher, Thomas, John, and Edward.

Henry Hudson married a woman named Katherine. They had three sons: Richard, John, and Oliver. John would sail with his father.

5

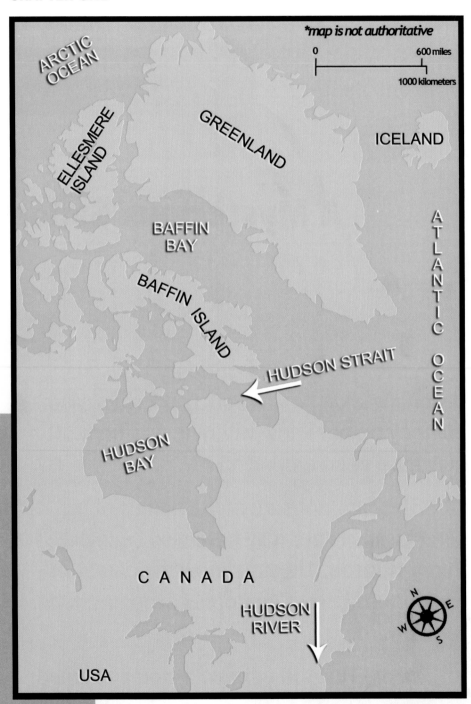

*map is not authoritative

ARCTIC OCEAN

ELLESMERE ISLAND

GREENLAND

ICELAND

BAFFIN BAY

BAFFIN ISLAND

HUDSON STRAIT

ATLANTIC OCEAN

HUDSON BAY

CANADA

HUDSON RIVER

USA

0 | 600 miles
1000 kilometers

On his third and fourth voyages, Henry Hudson explored parts of northeastern North America. He discovered waterways that would be called Hudson River, Hudson Bay, and Hudson Strait.

Hudson was a skilled sailor and a brave explorer. A sailor's life was not easy. Ships were small and the seas were dangerous. Sailors did not always return from their journeys.

No one knows how Hudson learned to sail, or who taught him how to **navigate** using the stars. He probably learned from his family or from other sailors. He may have worked as an **apprentice** aboard other sailing **vessels**.

More is known about his later life. Hudson wished to become a famous explorer. He sailed on the North Atlantic Ocean four times between 1607 and 1610. He was trying to find a northern route to the **Orient.** He wanted to go there to buy **spices,** silk, gems, and precious metals. Hudson thought he could sail over the North Pole. He did not know it was frozen.

He never found a passage over the pole to the Orient. But he did find what we now call Hudson River in New York. He also discovered Hudson **Bay** and Hudson **Strait** in Canada. He mapped and explored new lands. He became famous in his life and death.

Many ships that set sail to explore new lands wrecked at sea and never returned.

1607: First Voyage on the *Hopewell*

Henry Hudson and his English crew of 11 men set sail on May 1, 1607. They worked for the Muscovy Company. The Muscovy Company wanted to trade goods in the Orient. Henry Hudson's grandfather may have been one of the men who started this company. His name may have been Henry, too.

Hudson's wooden sailboat was called the *Hopewell.* It was not a fancy boat. It was small, and the men were crowded on it. His son John, who was 12, worked on the boat as a **cabin boy.**

Hudson and his men hoped to find a straight passage across the North Pole. The summer sun shone on the pole all day. Explorers thought the warm sun would melt the ice.

They sailed north of Scotland. Then they set sail for Greenland. They traveled toward islands that were north of the **Arctic** Circle.

Hudson and his crew met terrible conditions. They sailed through icy fog. Ice covered the ropes on the ship. The men's clothing got wet and froze. The ice cut and tore their hands.

After almost two months, Hudson had sailed farther north than any other sailor. The ship stopped less than 600 miles from the North Pole. Ice blocked the way. Hudson ordered his crew to turn around.

Hudson did not find a **Northwest Passage.** But he and his crew found whales. His discovery was the start of the English **whaling** industry. Hudson made money for the Muscovy Company. He and his crew returned to England on September 15, 1607.

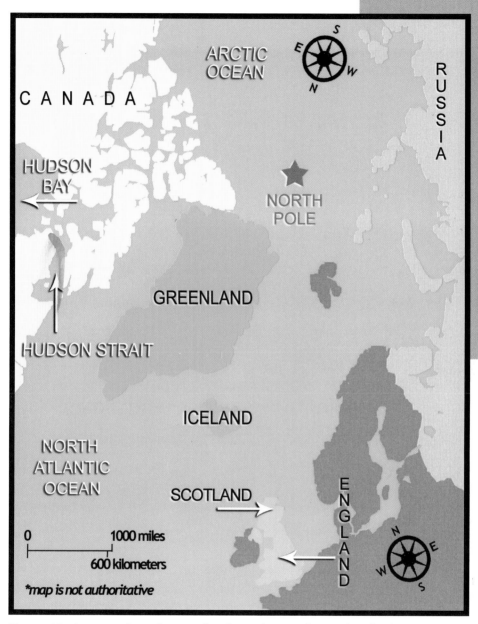

Henry Hudson explored many lands and seas during his four voyages. On his first voyage, he tried to sail from England to the North Pole. He planned to sail over the top of the world, then to the Orient, which is east and south of Russia. As the two compasses on the map show, to get anywhere from the North Pole, one has to sail south.

Henry Hudson often had to dodge huge icebergs. Only a fraction of the iceberg floats above the water. The rest of it is hidden below the surface.

1608: Second Voyage on the *Hopewell*

After his first try, Henry Hudson did not give up. He wanted to search for the passage again. The Muscovy Company paid for a second voyage. The company used money made from Hudson's whale discovery to pay for another trip.

On the first trip a year earlier, the *Hopewell* sailed north and west. This time, Hudson changed his course. He would go north, but then he would turn east. He planned to sail along the northern coast of Russia.

For this journey, the body, or hull, of the *Hopewell* was made stronger to protect it from the ice. On April 22, Hudson, his son John, and 13 other men left London. One sailor was Robert Juet. As a sailor, he did not like taking orders from Captain Hudson.

The three main parts of a sailing ship are its hull, mast, and sails. The hull of the *Hopewell* was made stronger to prevent damage in icy waters.

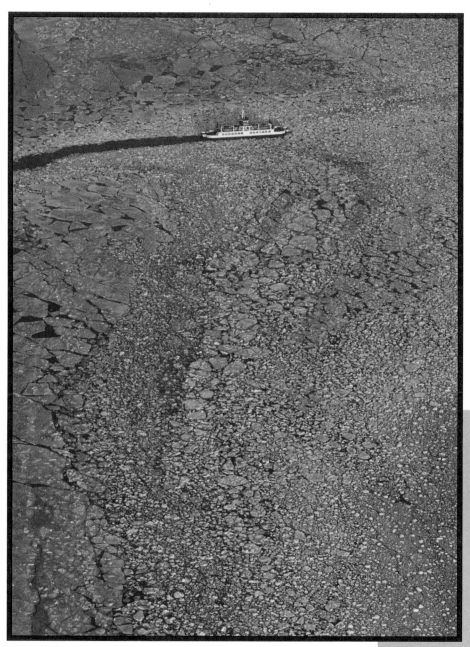

Modern icebreakers clear passages through icy waters. When Henry Hudson sailed, he had to navigate around ice. Sometimes his crew would use long poles to push the ice away from their small boat. It was dangerous work.

Again, the *Hopewell* ran into ice. The crew pushed it away from the boat with oars and poles. The cold, damp weather made them sick.

On June 15, two sailors saw something in the water. It had a woman's body and a porpoise's tail. They thought it was a **mermaid.** No one knows what the men really saw.

The *Hopewell* reached two islands north of Russia. The crew looked for water and food. Hudson looked for a way around the ice-locked islands. There was none.

The crew wanted to go home. Juet turned the men against Hudson. They became very angry. The crew threatened to **mutiny**, or to take over the ship.

Hudson returned to England on August 26, 1608. He had failed to find the passage through the polar region. The Muscovy Company was disappointed in him. There would be no more money. They were convinced there was no **Northeast** Passage.

Sometimes sailors saw things in the water that weren't really there. Two sailors on Hudson's *Hopewell* thought they saw a mermaid—a figure with a woman's body and a porpoise's tail.

Sailing for the Dutch East India Company, Henry Hudson and his crew set sail on the *Half Moon* on April 6, 1609. Robert Juet was again on the crew. No one knows why Hudson kept hiring him even after all the trouble he caused.

1609: Voyage on the *Half Moon*

Henry Hudson wanted to explore again. The English would not pay for another trip. He decided to sail for the Dutch East India Company from Amsterdam, Holland. The Dutch also wanted to trade with the people from the Orient. Hudson was ordered to repeat his last route, but he studied other routes too.

The *Half Moon* left Amsterdam on April 6, 1609. Hudson's crew was Dutch and English. Robert Juet sailed again. The Dutch and English did not get along. They did not

England's Captain John Smith sent Henry Hudson a letter about a passage to Asia through America. Smith had sailed to America in 1606. He helped establish the colony of Jamestown. Hudson and his crew would sail to America because of Smith's letter.

speak the same language. The Dutch did not expect the ice and cold. After weeks of sailing in freezing weather, they refused to go farther.

Hudson shared a letter he had from another famous explorer, Captain John Smith. Smith wrote about a passage through America. The crew agreed to try it. They set sail for America.

The *Half Moon* reached America on July 17. The sailors met Penobscot Indians in Maine. Hudson traded beads for furs. The crew did not trust the Indians. Before leaving Maine, Juet and some of the crew robbed them.

The *Half Moon* sailed south to North Carolina and then turned north again. They looked for the passage. Hudson entered New York Harbor and traded goods with the Lenape Indians. On September 6, the Indians attacked five men. One died.

Hudson took two Indian prisoners. They escaped. Hudson sailed up a river that would

In 1609, the *Half Moon* sailed into the mouth of what would be called the Hudson River in New York State. Henry Hudson and his crew were met there by Native Americans.

be named for him: the Hudson River. He visited with the Mohawk Indians.

The river became shallow. This was not the Northwest Passage. On October 4, he sailed back into the Atlantic Ocean. He headed to England and not Amsterdam. Hudson did not want to face the Dutch. He had disobeyed orders.

Henry Hudson and his crew attacked a Native American village along the Hudson River. He took two natives as prisoners.

In 1611, on his fourth voyage to find a northern route to the Orient by water, angry sailors forced Henry Hudson, his son John, and seven other crew members into a small boat.

1610–1611: Voyage on the *Discovery*

Hudson once again sailed for the British. This time, he was given command of the *Discovery,* a sturdy sailing vessel. He planned to sail north of England and then west of Greenland.

He selected 23 men. The man who had caused trouble before—Robert Juet—was one of them. Hudson's son John was also part of the crew. The boat set sail on April 17. Soon there was trouble again. Bad weather stopped the boat. The crew grew restless and fought. Juet told rumors about Hudson.

The ship passed the southern tip of Greenland and sailed west. Hudson tried to enter Furious Overfall, now called Hudson Strait. The ship dodged ice. The men became

Explorer Henry Hudson tries to comfort his son John. After a mutiny by Hudson's crew, nine members of the *Discovery* were left to die in a shallop in the icy waters of Hudson Bay.

scared. They refused to sail and wanted to go home. Hudson wanted to go farther west.

They entered a large bay. It would become known as Hudson Bay. Hudson thought it was the Pacific Ocean. He thought he was close to the Orient. He looked for a passage south. His crew became angry. Juet led a protest.

Ice **floes** filled the bay. The ship was stuck. Hudson and his crew camped for seven months in cold, wintry weather. They hunted and fished. They became hungry and sick.

In spring, they sailed again. The crew thought they were going home, but Hudson continued to search for the passage.

On June 22, angry sailors put Hudson, his son John, and seven of his loyal sailors in a small boat called a **shallop**. Hudson and his men drifted away from the *Discovery*. They were never seen or heard from again.

Nine men and the *Discovery* returned to England on October 20, 1611. Several years later, they were found not guilty of mutiny.

CHRONOLOGY

1570(?)   Henry Hudson is born in England.

1607   Hudson sets sail on the *Hopewell,* discovers whales but no northern passage, and returns to England.

1608   Hudson sets sail on the *Hopewell* for a second voyage, explores the northern coast of Russia but finds no passage, and returns to England.

1609   Hudson sails for the Dutch on the *Half Moon,* explores North America, discovers the Hudson River but no passage, and returns to England.

1610   Hudson sails for the British aboard the *Discovery,* explores Canada, and discovers Hudson Strait and Hudson Bay.

1611   Hudson and his *Discovery* crew are trapped in ice in Hudson Bay and camp out for seven months; in June, he, his son John, and loyal crew members are set adrift in the *Discovery* 's shallop, never to be seen again.

Fall 1611   The remaining *Discovery* crew returns to England.

1613   Two English ships are sent to look for a northern passage and for Henry Hudson and his crew.

1618   *Discovery* crew members that were involved in the mutiny are found not guilty.

TIMELINE IN HISTORY

1497	John Cabot searches for the Northwest Passage. He possibly enters Hudson Bay.
1524	Giovanni da Verrazano searches for the passage; he discovers New York Bay.
1576	English explorer Martin Frobisher thinks he discovers the passage, but it is a Canadian bay.
1577–1580	Francis Drake sails around the world.
1584	Fleming Oliver Brunel searches for the Northeast Passage.
1587	England's John Davis discovers Davis Strait, which separates Canada and Greenland.
1594–1596	Dutchman Willem Barents searches for the Northeast Passage, starting from Asia.
1602	George Weymouth, in the *Discovery,* reaches Hudson Strait.
1606	John Knight sails the *Hopewell* in search of the Northwest Passage.
1612–1613	Thomas Button searches for Henry Hudson and the passage.
1614	Benjamin Joseph and William Baffin take thirteen ships in search of the Northeast Passage.
1728	Danish navigator Vitus Bering discovers the Bering Strait.
1737–1850	Dozens of expeditions, including several overland journeys, set out to find the passage.
1850–1854	British naval officer Robert McClure discovers the final link in the Northwest Passage.

FIND OUT MORE

Books

Dreher, Diane Sansevere. *Explorers Who Got Lost.* New York: Tor, 1992.

Goodman, Joan. *Beyond the Sea of Ice: Voyages of Henry Hudson.* New York: Mikaya Press, 1999.

West, Tracy. *Voyage of the* Half Moon. New York: Silver Moon Press, 1993.

Works Consulted

Asher, G.M., Ll.D. *Henry Hudson the Navigator: The Original Documents in Which His Career Is Recorded, Collected, Partly Translated, and Annotated.* New York: Burt Franklin, 1964.

DeCosta, B.F., Reverend. *Sailing Directions of Henry Hudson, Prepared for His Use in 1608.* Albany: Joel Munsell, 1869.

Edwards, Philip. *Last Voyages: Cavendish, Hudson, Raleigh: The Original Narratives.* Oxford: Clarendon Press, 1988.

Hamilton, Milton W. *Henry Hudson and the Dutch in New York.* Albany: The University of the State of New York, 1959.

Harmon, Daniel. *The Hudson River.* Philadelphia: Chelsea House, 2004.

Janvier, Thomas A. *Henry Hudson: A Brief Statement of His Aims and His Achievements.* New York and London: Harper & Brothers Publishers, 1909.

Johnson, Donald S. *Charting the Sea of Darkness: The Four Voyages of Henry Hudson.* Camden, Maine: McGraw Hill/International Marine, 1993.

Millman, Lawrence. "Looking for Henry Hudson," *Smithsonian Magazine,* October 1999.

On the Internet

Chadwick, Ian. *The Life and Voyages of Henry Hudson, English Explorer and Navigator,* © 1992–2005.
http://www.ianchadwick.com/hudson

Half Moon Replica and New Netherland Museum
http://www.newnetherland.org

Hudson River Maritime Museum, "Henry Hudson and Early Hudson River History"
http://www.hrmm.org/halfmoon/halfmoon.htm

PBS: "Empire of the Bay: Henry Hudson"
http://www.pbs.org/empireofthebay/profiles/hudson.html

GLOSSARY

apprentice (ah-PREN-tiss)—someone who learns a craft by working with someone skilled in that area.

Arctic (ARK-tik)—frozen area around the North Pole.

bay—a part of the ocean that is partially surrounded by land.

cabin boy—a young boy who does chores on a ship.

floe—large flat sheet of floating ice.

historian (his-TOR-ee-en)—someone who studies the past, or history.

mermaid (MER-mayd)—a mythical figure described as having the head and body of a woman and the tail of a porpoise.

mutiny (MEW-tih-nee)—a revolt by a ship's crew against its captain.

navigate (NAA-vih-gayt)—to plot and then follow a ship's course.

Northeast Passage—a sea route connecting the Atlantic Ocean to the Pacific Ocean by way of the northern coasts of Europe and Asia.

Northwest Passage—a sea route connecting the Atlantic Ocean to the Pacific Ocean by way of the northern coast of North America.

Orient (OR-ee-ent)—the eastern part of Asia, mainly China and Japan.

shallop (SHAH-lup)—a small boat with oars, used in shallow waters and often for exploring.

spices—fragrant plants used to flavor foods.

strait—a narrow strip of water connecting two larger bodies of water.

vessel—a ship or boat.

whaling—the hunting of whales for their meat, oil, and bones.

INDEX